Violin Online String Sampler

Piano Accompaniment

By Robin Kay Deverich

Global Music School String Publications

Graphic Design by Julia Kay

ISBN 9780982170519

http://www.violinonlinestringsampler.com

TABLE OF CONTENTS

CLASSICAL PERIOD

ROMANTIC PERIOD

20th CENTURY

NON-TRADITIONAL

Preface

Violin Online String Sampler Piano Accompaniment features the piano accompaniment to *Violin Online String Sampler Violin Sheet Music* (sold separately). 54 pieces are included in this collection, representing styles from a variety of music history periods and cultures, including Medieval, Renaissance, Baroque, Classical, Romantic, 20th Century, Fiddle, Klezmer, Gypsy, Chinese, Greek, Carnatic, Arabic, Mariachi, Ragtime and Blues. These arrangements include a representative sampling of most major forms of string music such as concertos, symphonies, sonatas, quartets and trios. A study guide, sold separately, explains the history and musical form of the selected pieces, and includes violin technique tips for each piece of music.

As an added bonus, sound files of each piece are currently available on a website* specifically designed to accompany this course: *http://www.violinonlinestringsampler.com.* Content from ViolinOnline™ is also provided on this site, including a review of violin basics such as instrument care and tuning; violin playing position; fingering assistance; violin technique tips; scales and etudes; and music theory basics.

Making music can bring you joy, and this string sampler is designed to help you actively learn, study and play beautiful string music from a wide variety of styles and eras. Let the music begin!

**No guarantees are made that these sound files and website will be available indefinitely.*

Columba aspexit

Hildegard

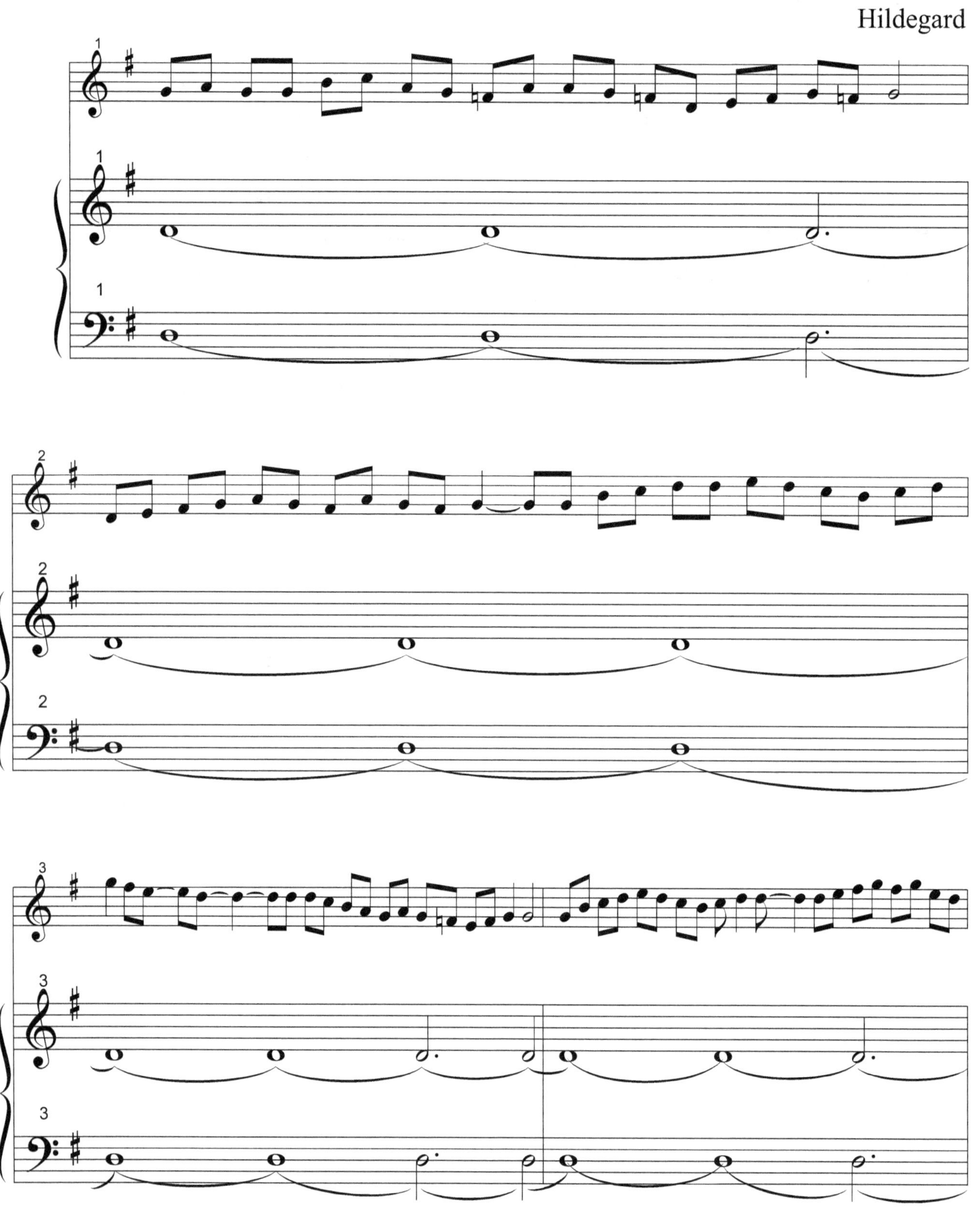

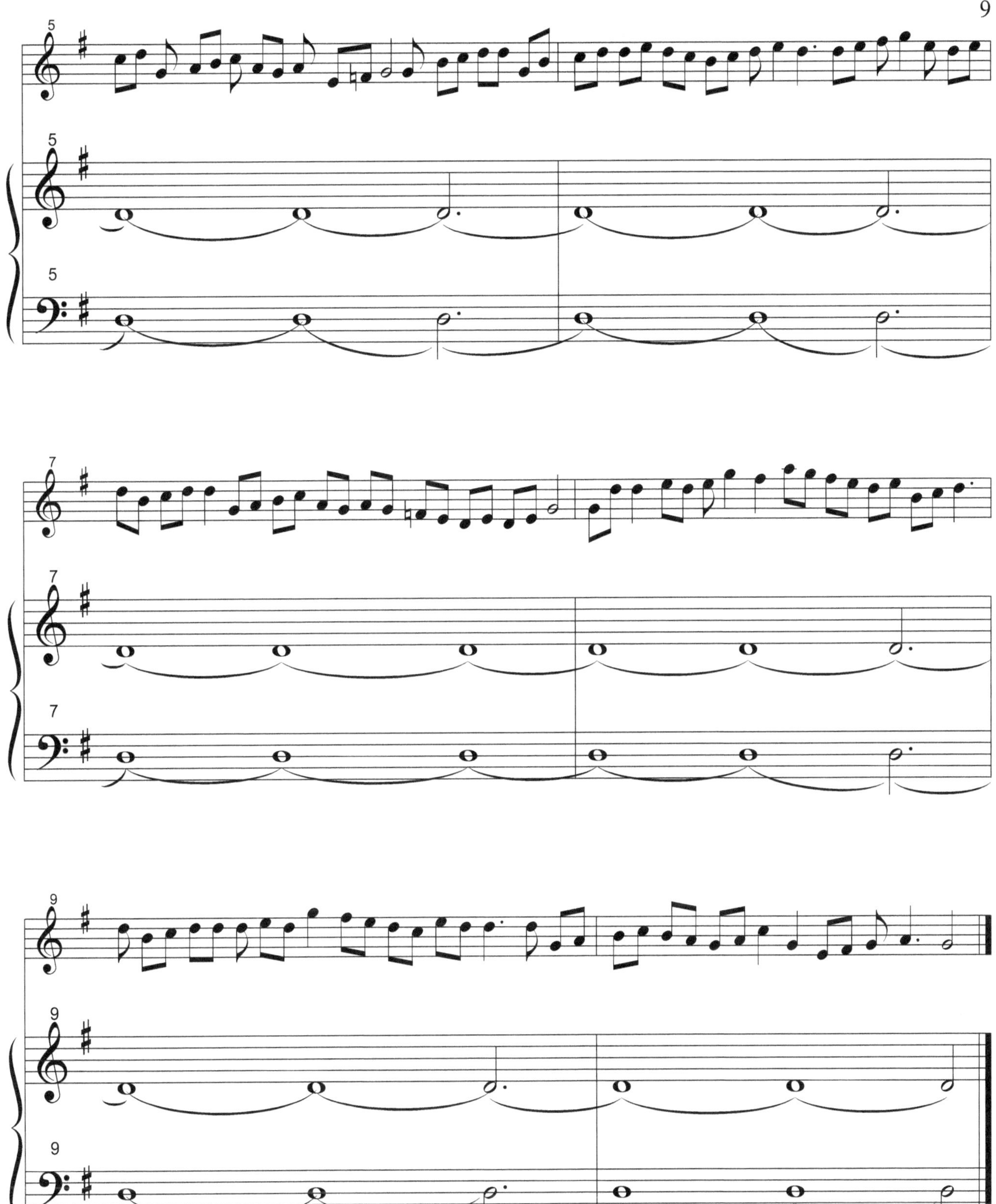
5
5
5
7
7
7
9
9
9

Sixth Royal Estampie

Anonymous

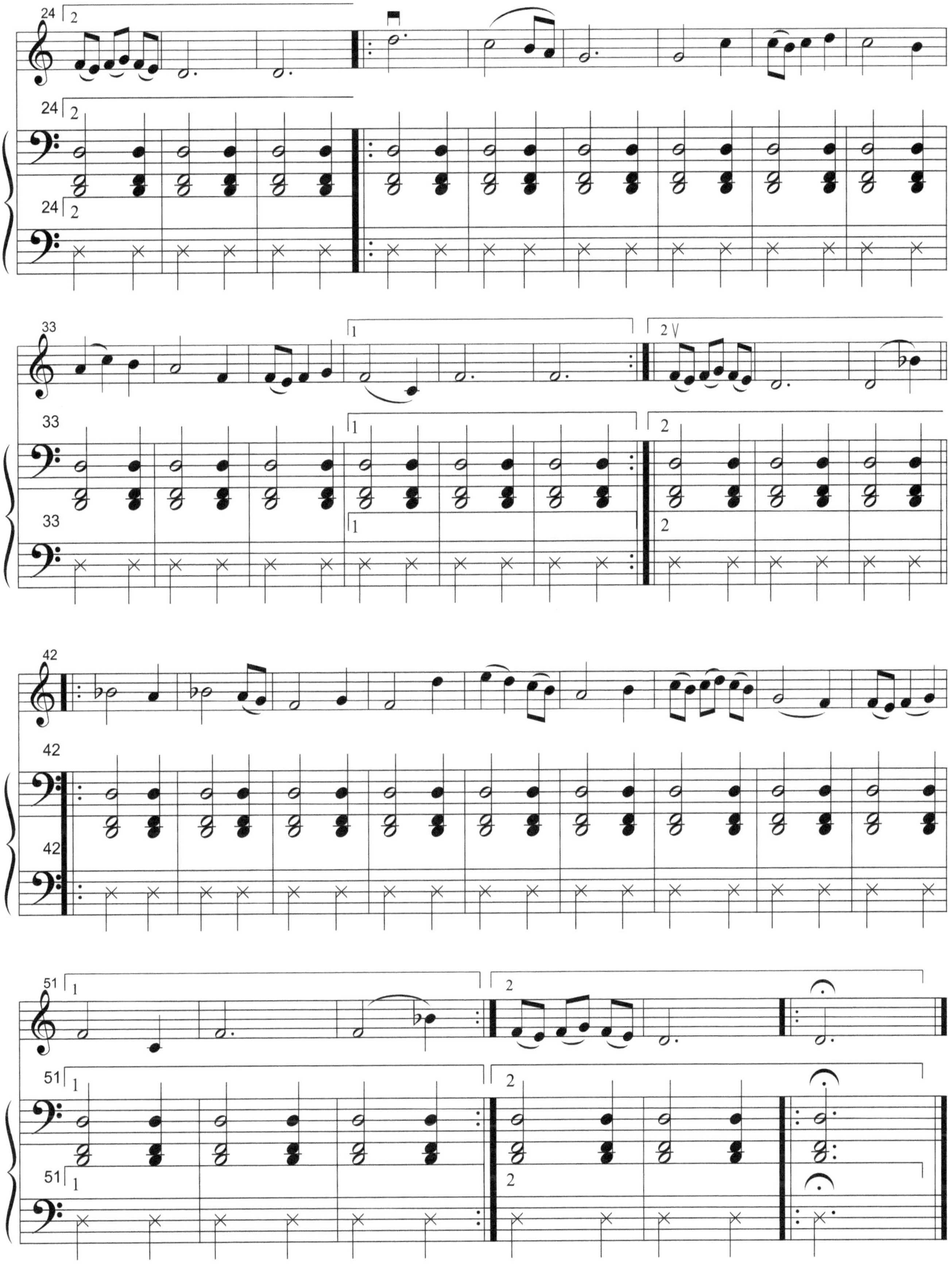

Helas madame

Henry VIII

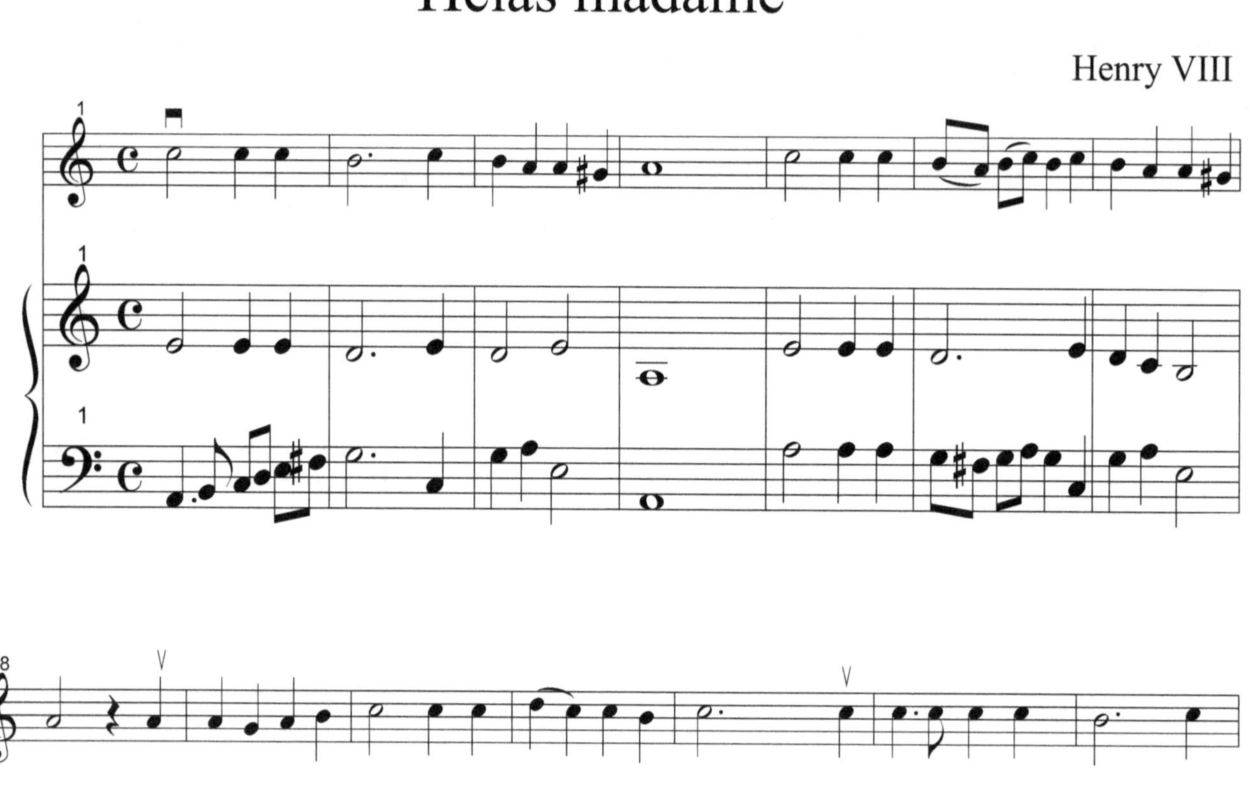

Kemp's Jigg

Anonymous

Fantasia

Lupo

6

6

11

11

16
16
20
20
24
24

Minuet 1

Crome

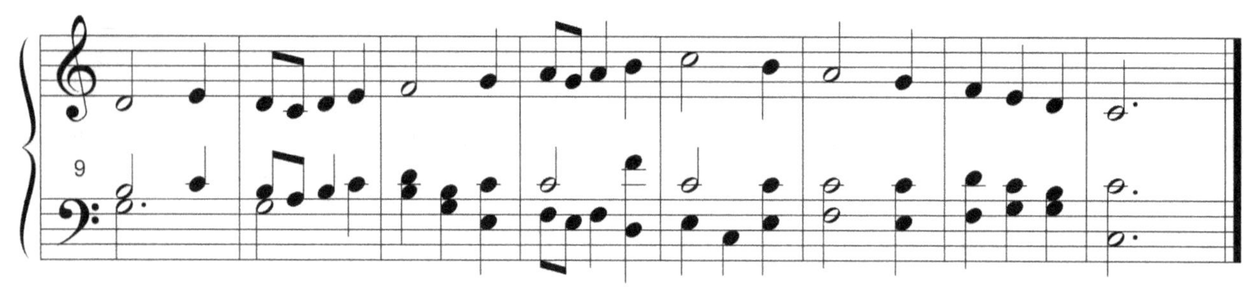

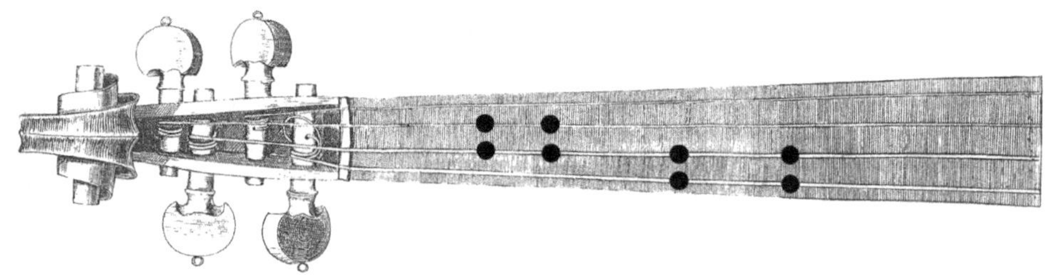

Robert Crome Violin Fingerboard & Minuet

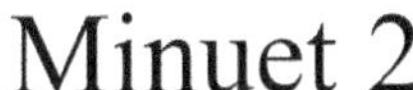

Minuet 2

Crome

Minuet 3

Crome

Minuet 4

Crome

Minuet 5

Crome

Rondeau

Purcell

13
13
13

16
16
16

19
19
19

30
30
30

Hornpipe

from Water Music Suite in D

Handel

14
14
14

18
18
18

22
22
22

27
27
27
31
31
31
35
35
35

La Folia

Marais La Folia theme

Marais Variation 1

Corelli Variation 2

Vivaldi Variation 3

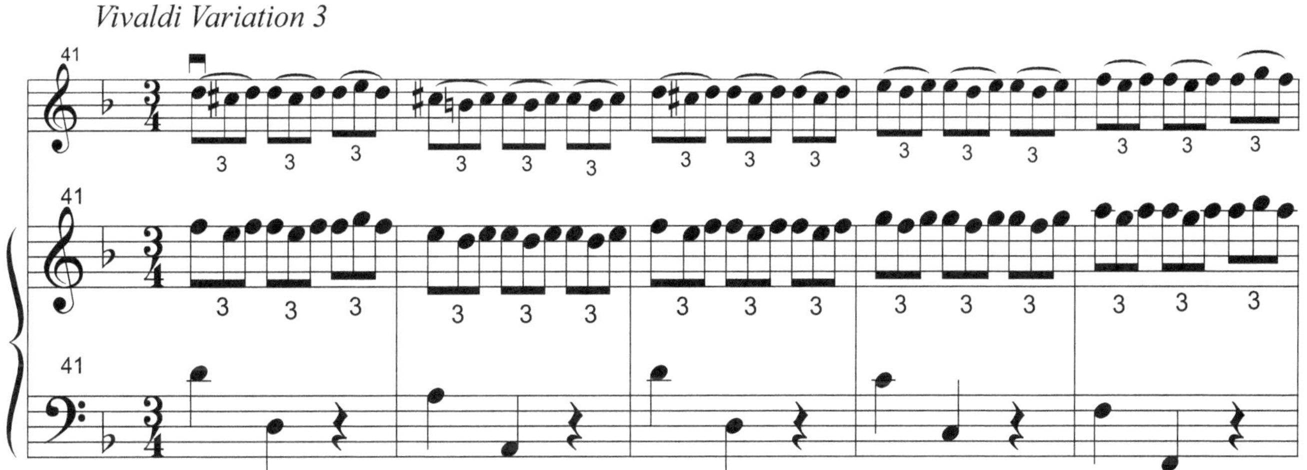

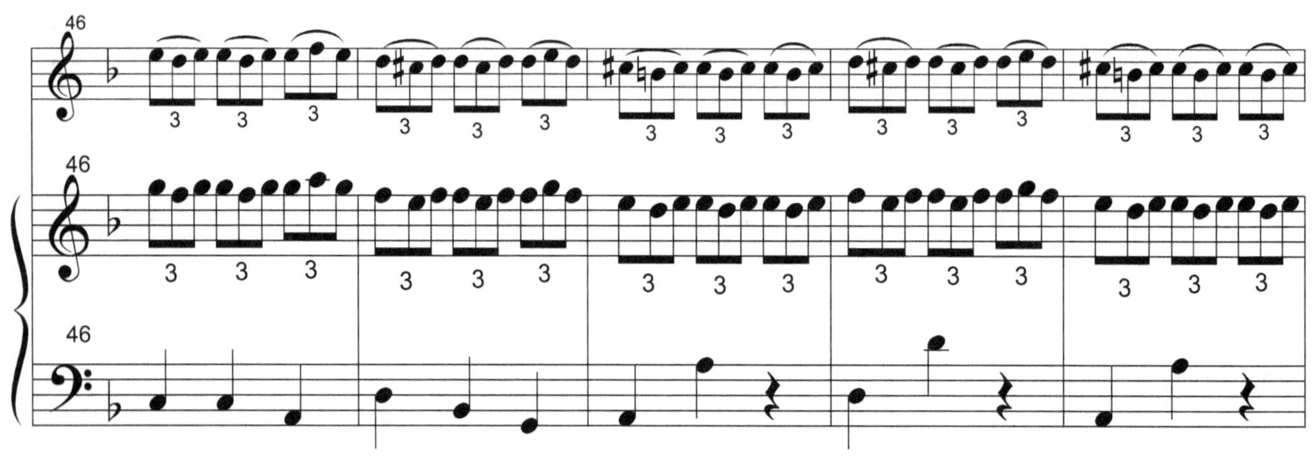

Corelli Variation 4

61
61
61
65
65
65
69
69
69

Violin Concerto in A minor

1st Movement

Vivaldi

10
10
10

13
13
13

16
16
16

19
19
19
22
22
22
25
25
25

28
28
28
31
31
31
34
34
34

Prelude

from Cello Suite No. 1

Bach

25
28
31
34
37
40
43
46

Allegro

from Brandenburg Concerto No. 5

Bach

9
9
9
9

13
13
13
13

17
17
mf
17
mf
17

21
21
21
21

25
25
25
25

29
29
29
29

33
f
33
33
33

37
37
37
37

41
41
41
41

45
45
45
45

Kyrie

Cazzati

19
19
19

25
25
25

31
31
31

55
55
55

60
60
60

65
65
65

Messiah

He Shall Feed His Flock

Handel

Hallelujah Chorus

38
38
38
38
41
41
41
41
44
44
44
44

47
47
47
47
50
50
50
50
52
52
52
52

54
57
60

Arioso

Bach

20
26
33

Ave Verum Corpus

Mozart

22
mp
22
mp
22
mp
29
cresc.
mf
cresc.
f
29
cresc.
mf
cresc.
f
29
cresc.
mf
cresc.
f
36
dim.
mp
36
dim.
mp
36
dim.
mp

Adagio

from Violin Concerto No. 3

Mozart

mp
mf
mf
tr

21
3
25
28

42
42
42
45
45
45
48
48
48
tr

51
51
51
54
tr
54
54
57
57
57

Andante

from String Quartet No. 13 in A minor

Schubert

12
f
mp
12
12

16
16
16

20
20
20

Andante

from the Emperor Quartet

Haydn

Poco Adagio Cantabile

16
16
16

21
21
21

25
25
25

29
29
29

33
33
33

37
37
37

Surprise Symphony

Haydn

Pastoral Symphony No. 6

Beethoven

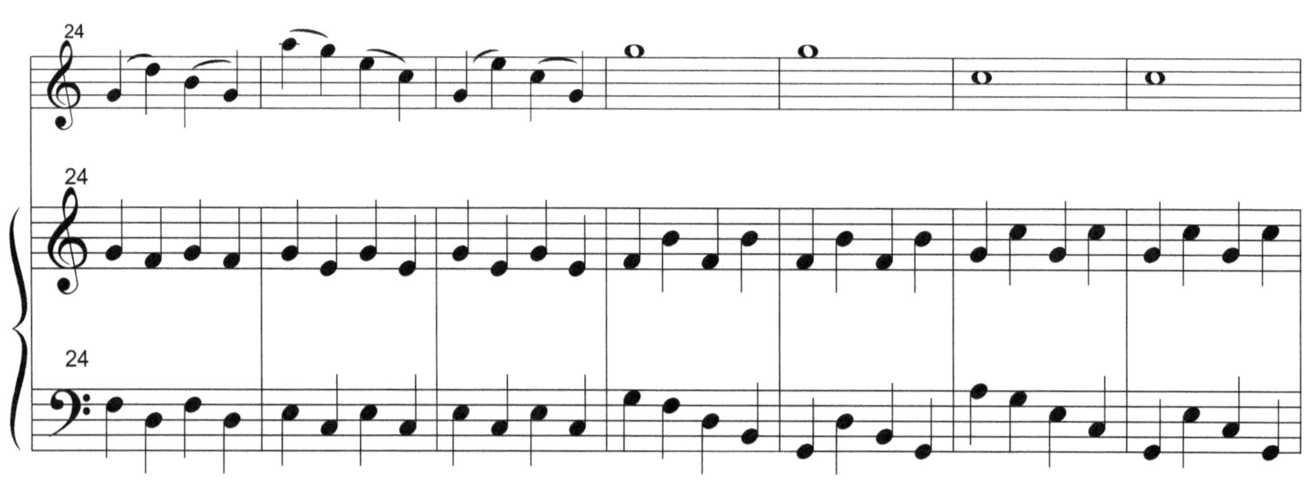

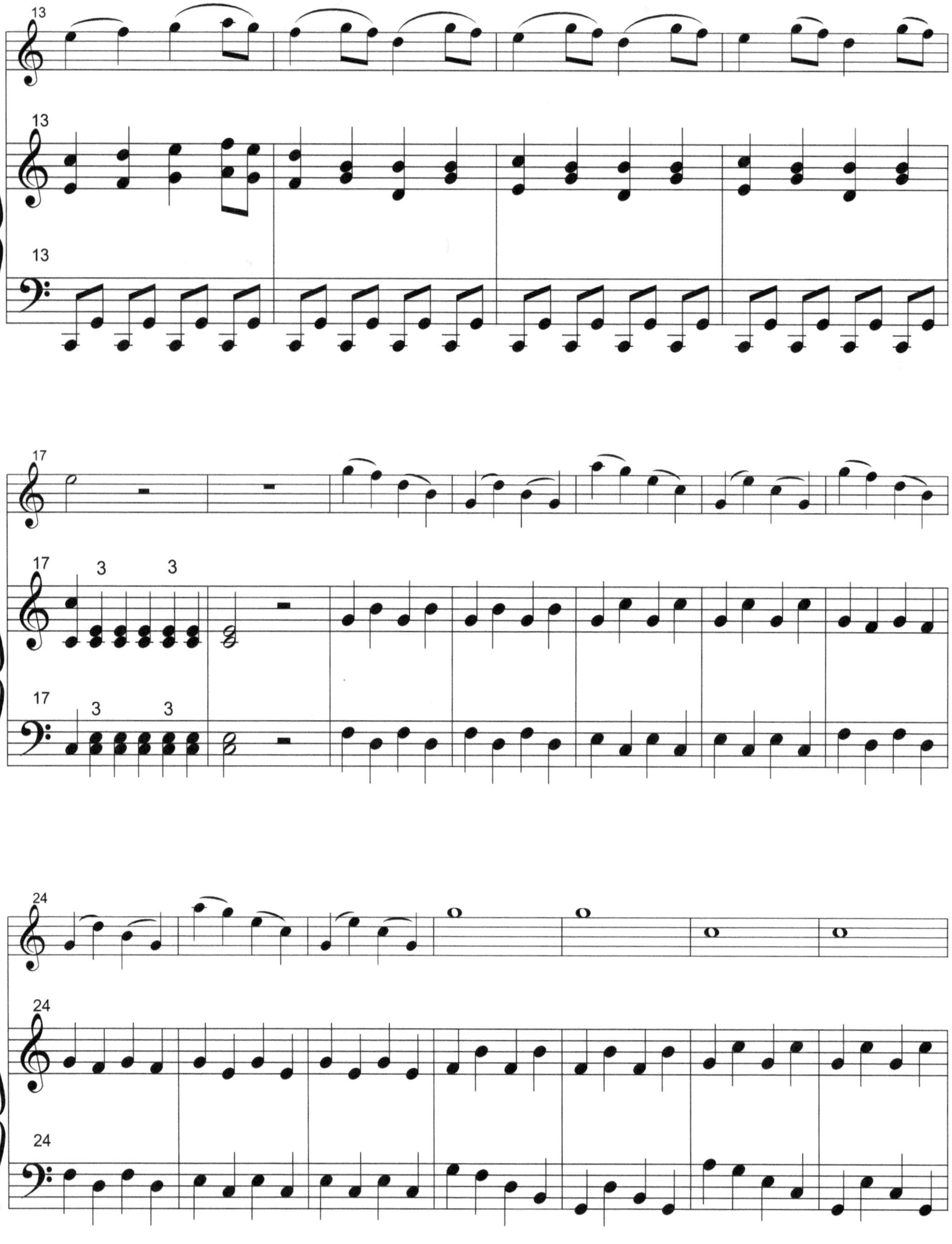
13
13
13
17
17
3
3
17
3
3
24
24
24

31
3
3
3
3
31
3
3
3
3
31
Scene by the brook
38
38
38
43
43
43

47
47
47
50
50
50
53
53
53

58
58
58

65
65
65

67
67
67

Hungarian Dance No. 5

Brahms

26
poco rit.
a tempo
mp
f
p poco rit.
a tempo f
35
Vivace
f
mf
43
poco rit.
a tempo
poco rit.
a tempo
2xD.C. al Coda
mp
p poco rit.
a tempo
poco rit.
a tempo
2x,D.C. al Coda
Coda
51
Coda

The Moldau

from Má vlast

Smetana

10
10
10
13
13
13
16
16
16

19
19
19

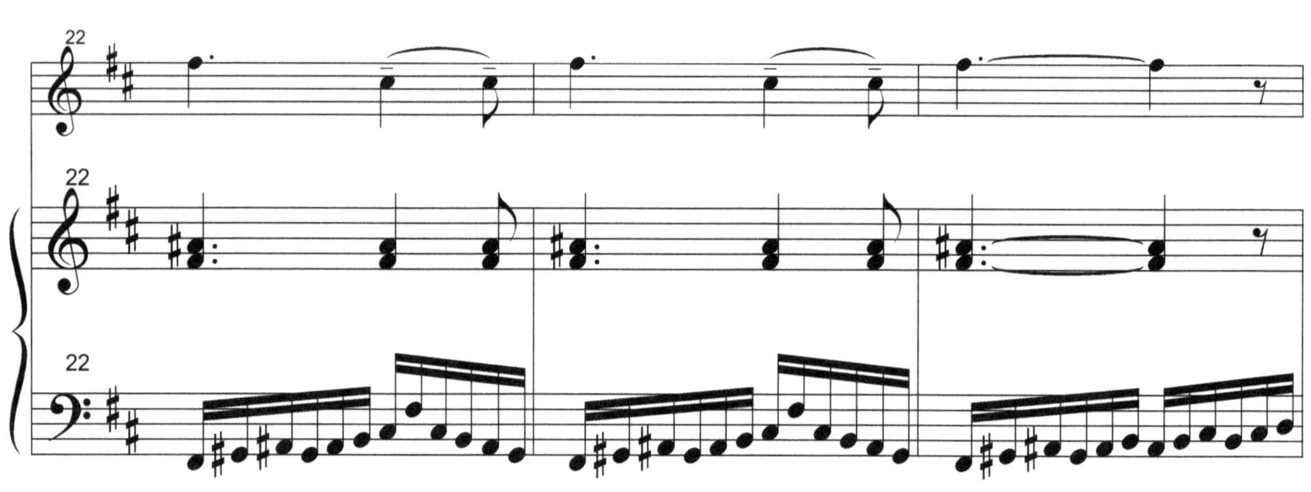
22
22
22

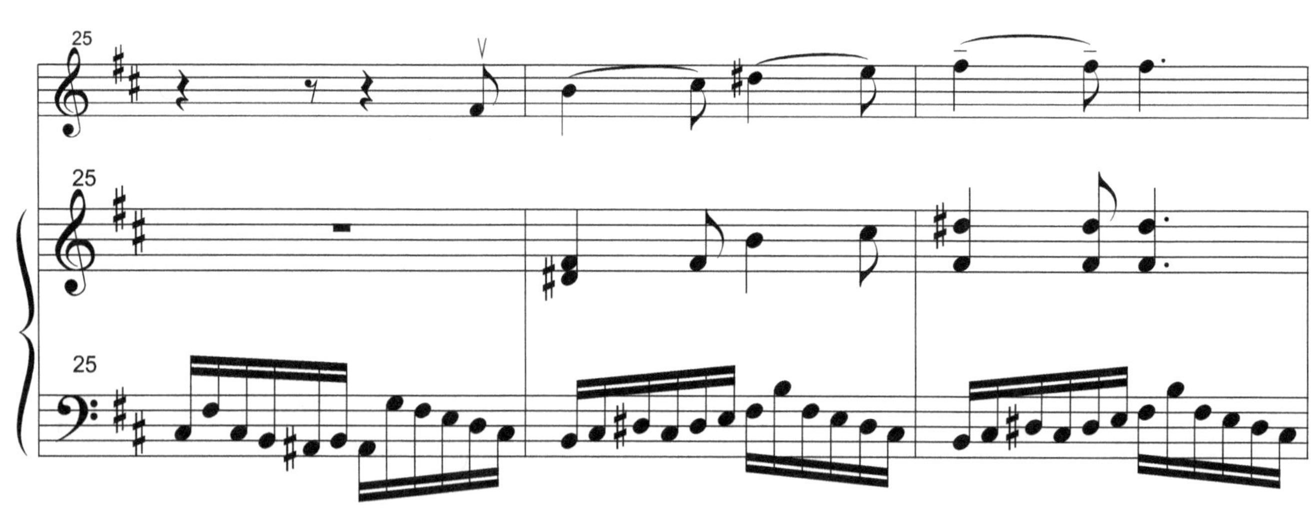
25
25
25

Halling

Grieg

18
18
18
23
23
23
28
28
28

Emperor Waltz

Strauss

25
25

33
33

41
41

Vieille Chanson

Allegretto

Viardot

16
16
16
21
f
p
cresc.
21
mf
p
cresc.
21
26
f
dim.
26
mf
dim.
26

30
mp
mf
30
p
34
mp
34
38
38
dim.

42
mp
p
46
cresc.
mf
cresc.
mp
50

54
cresc.
f
54
cresc.
mf
54
59
59
59
64
p
cresc.
mf
64
pp
cresc.
mp
64

68
68
68
72
72
72
76
76
76

Andante

from Violin Concerto Op. 64

Mendelssohn

28
28
28
33
33
33
38
38
38

Cello Concerto in B Minor

13
13
13

16
16
16

Adagio ma non troppo
20
20
20

molto espressivo e largamente
26
V
3
26
26
29
29
3
29
32
32
32

Nocturne

from String Quartet No. 2

Andante *cantabile ed espressivo*

Borodin

16
16
16
21
21
21
3
26
26
26
3

31
31
31
3

37
37
37
3

43
43
43

Elégie

15
15
15
19
19
19
23
23
23

26
26
26
30
30
30
34
34
34

Barcarolla

Vieuxtemps

19
19
19

24
24
24

29
29
29

Ave Maria

Andante semplice

Bach-Gounod

10
V
10

13
13

16
16

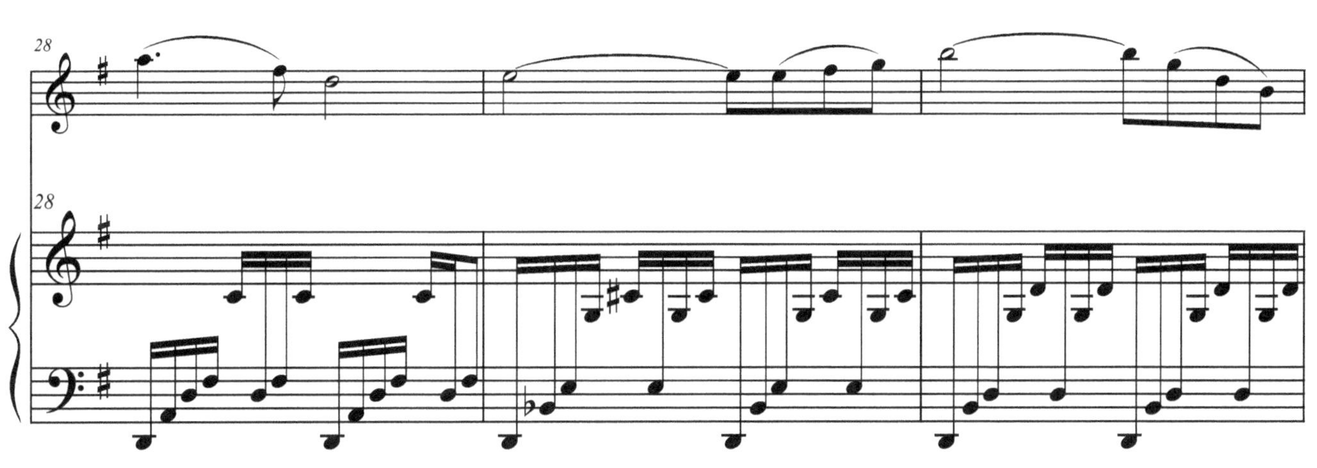
28
28

31
1
31
1

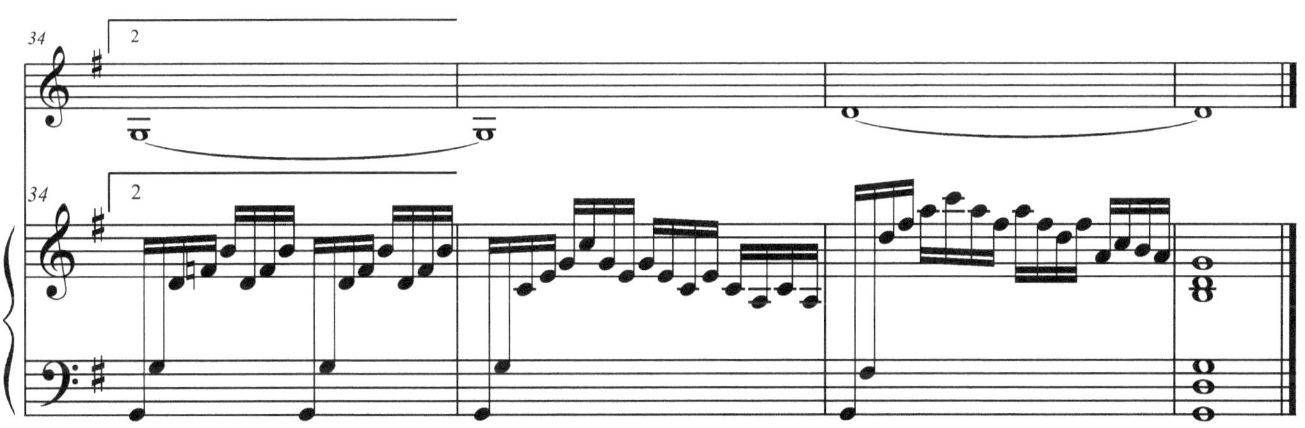
34
2
34
2

Sicilienne

Fauré

21
21
21

28
28
28

35
35
35

42
42
42

49
49
49

56
56
56

63
63
63

70
70
70

77
77
77

Meditation

from Thaïs

Massenet

13
f
3
3
3
dim.
3
3
3
mp
16
mp
rall.
a tempo piu mosso
20
mf
3
3

poco a poco appassionato
calmato
poco più appassionato
cresc.
più mosso agitato

34
sfz
sfz
rall.
dim.
34
34
a tempo
38
3
5
38
38
42
rall.
42
42

a tempo
46
3
46
46
49
cresc.
f
3
3
dim.
3
3
49
49
52
3
3
cresc.
rall.
52
52

a tempo
56
cresc.
sfz
dim.
mp
60
3
64
3
calmato
3
sfz
dim.
p
f

Habanera

Bizet

21
21
3
3
3
21

26
26
26

31
31
31
35
35
35
39
39
39
3

Dance of the Reed Flutes

from The Nutcracker Suite

Tchaikovsky

17
17
17
22
D.C. al Coda
22
D.C. al Coda
22
Coda
26
3
3
Coda
26
3
26

Overture

from Pulcinella

Stravinsky

10
13
16

19
19
19
22
22
22
25
25
25

28
28
28
31
31
31
34
34
34

37
37
37
40
40
40
43
43
43

Trio Sonata No. 1

(originally attributed to Pergolesi)

Gallo

Moderato

11
11
11
15
15
15
19
19
19

23
23
23

27
27
27

30
30
30

34
34
34

37
37
37

40
40
40

Assez vif

from Quartet in F

Ravel

11
p
3
3
11
pp
11
14
3
14
14
17
3
mf
3
17
mf
17

20

3

20

20

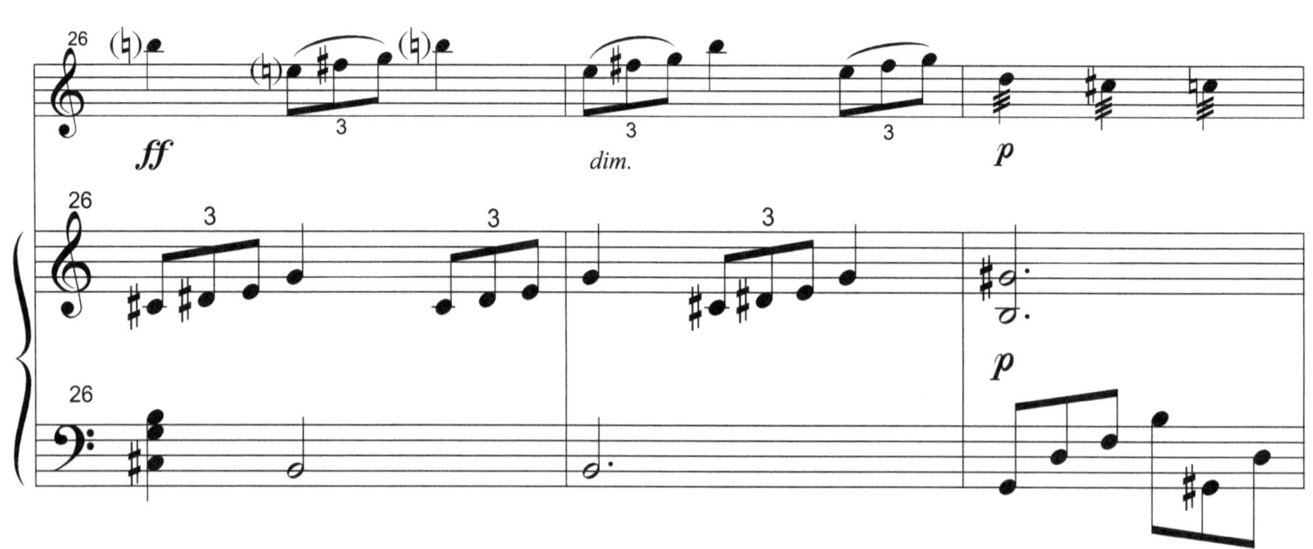

pizz.
cresc.
mf
cresc.
mf
f
p
ff
f
p
f

Sehr langsam

from 4 Pieces, Op. 7

Webern

Simple Gifts

Brackett

Braul

Bartok

16
16
16
22
5
22
22
28
28
28

The Basso

Gypsy Traditional

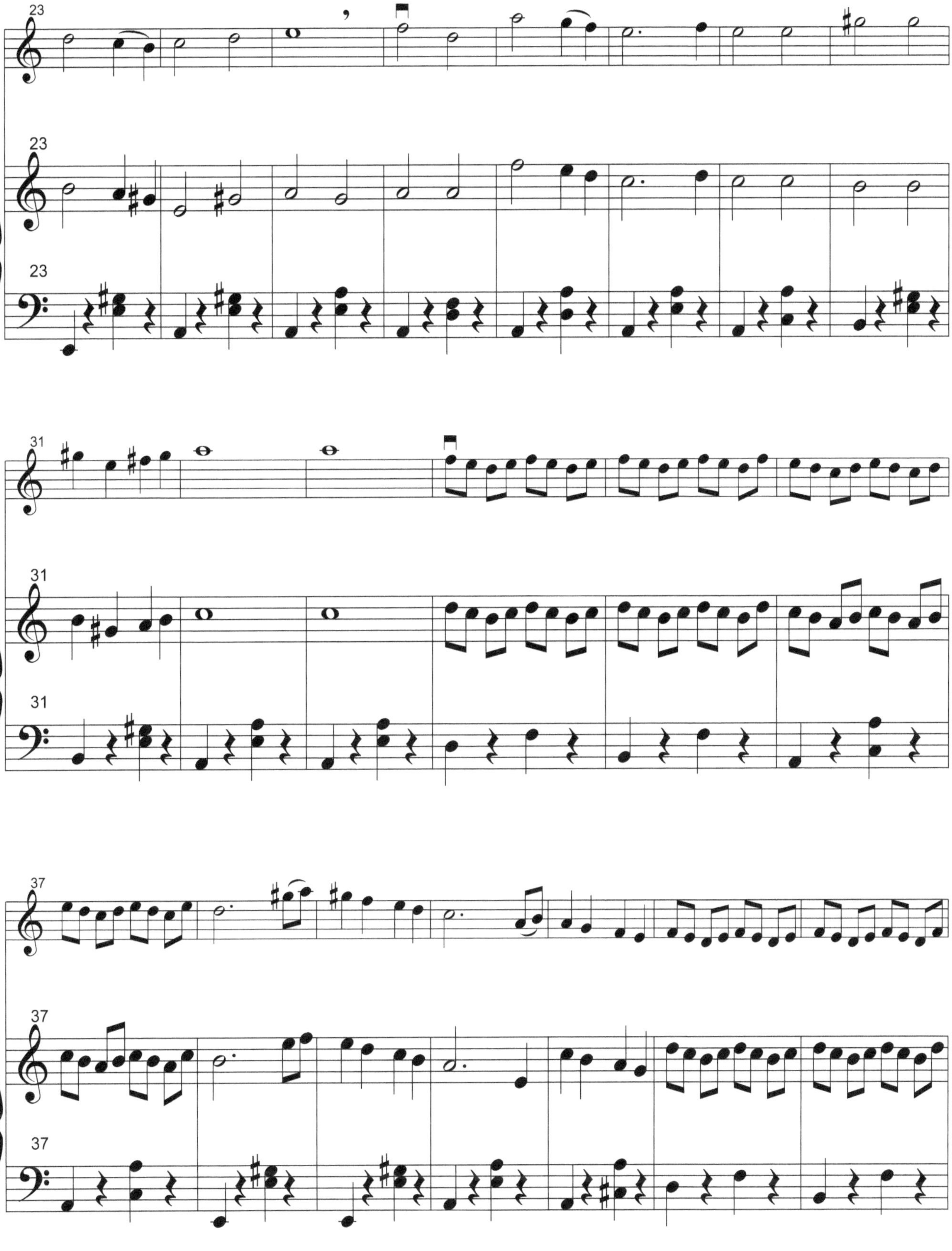

Odessa Bulgarish

Klezmer Traditional

22
22
22
29
29
29
36
36
36

43
43
43
50
50
50
57
57
57

Varys Hasapikos

Andante

Greek Traditional

21
21

26
26

31
31

36
36

El jarabe tapatío

Mexican Traditional

19
19
19

25
25
25

31
31
31

37
37
37

42
42
42

47
47
47

Jasmine Flower

Chinese Traditional

13
13
13

18
18
18

23
rit.
23
rit.
23

Sara Sara

Tyagaraja

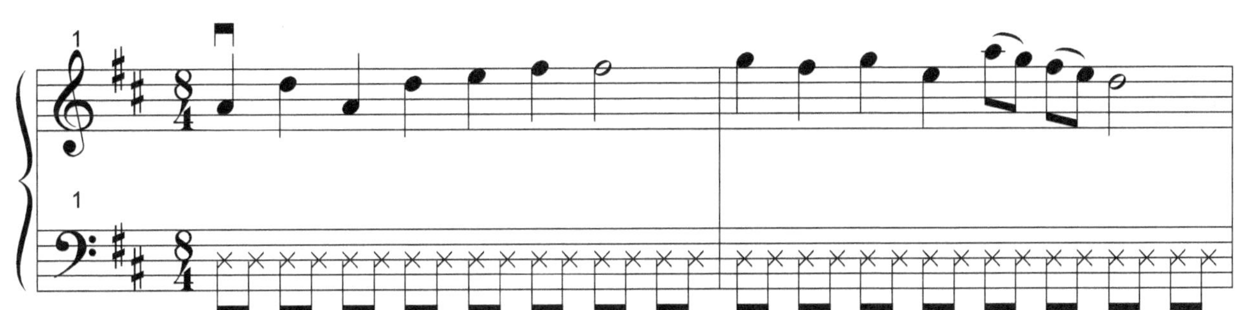

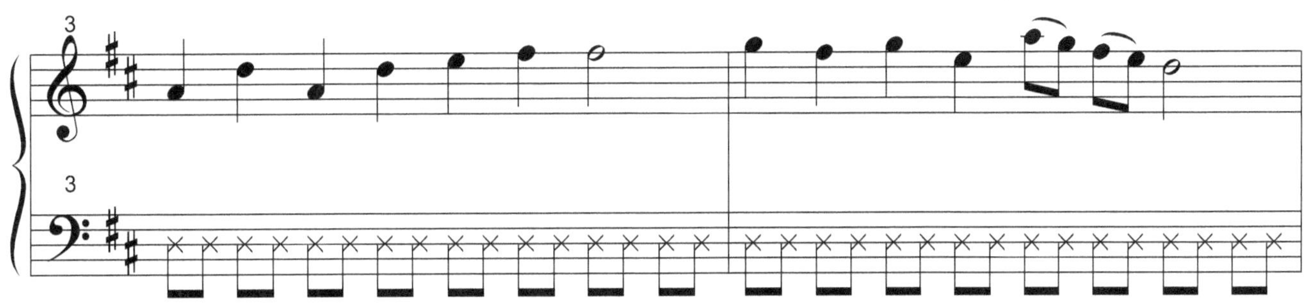

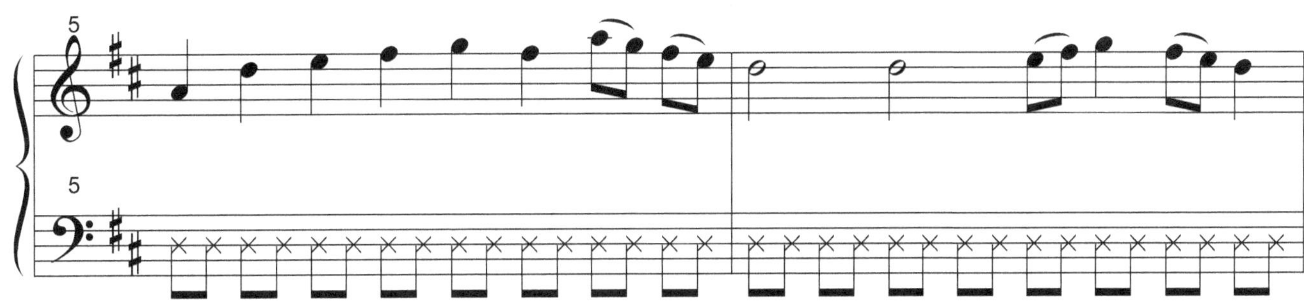

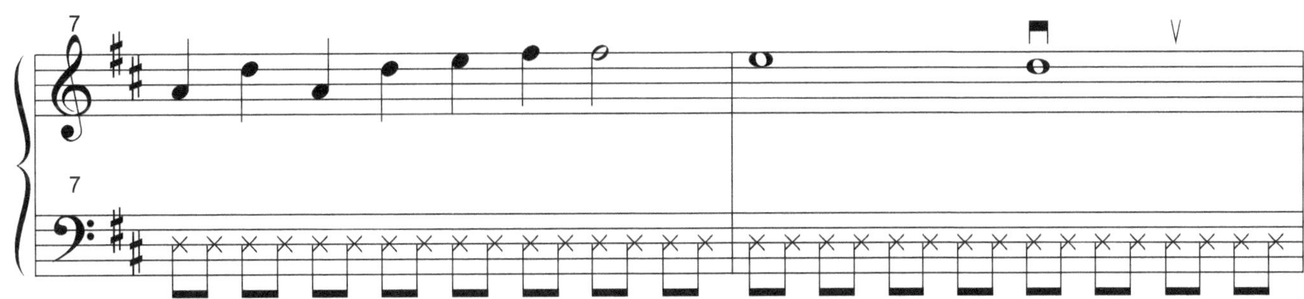

9
9
12
12
15
15
18
18
21
21

23
23
25
25
27
27
29
29
31
31

Longa Nahawand

Bey

21
21
25
25
29
29
33
33
37
37

Fiddle Medley

Irish Washerwoman

Irish Traditional

Ragtime Violin

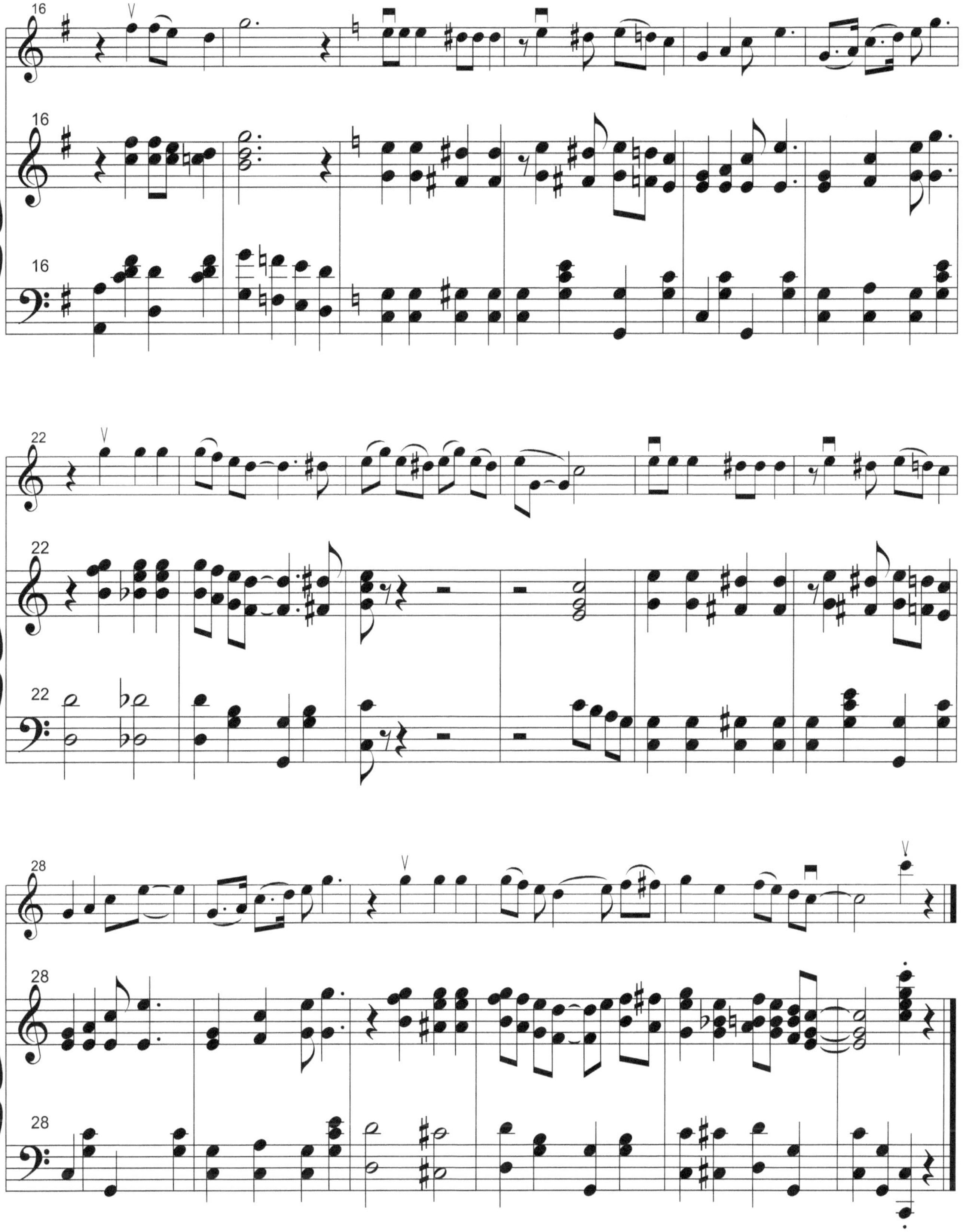

The Castle Walk

Europe & Dabney

24
24
24
32
32
32
39
39
39

47
47
47
53
53
53
60
60
60

67
75
82

90
90
90
97
97
97
103
103
103

109
109
109
116
116
116
122
122
122
8va
8vb

St. Louis Blues

Handy

16
16
16

21
21
21

25
25
25

29
29
29

33
33
33

37
37
37

41
41
41

45
45
45

49
49
49

www.ingramcontent.com/pod-product-compliance
Lightning Source LLC
LaVergne TN
LVHW061246100826
845148LV00008B/1038
* 9 7 8 0 9 8 2 1 7 0 5 1 9 *